Richarc

Chippenham
in old picture postcards

by Terence J. Griffiths

European Library *ZALTBOMMEL/THE NETHERLANDS*

GB ISBN 90 288 2554 1

Third revised edition, 1983.

INTRODUCTION

In A.D. 853, Ethelswitha, sister of the legendary King Alfred, was married to the King of Mercia in the town of Chippenham. This is the first reference to the little town nestling in the thick forest of Wessex. In 878 a less happy event is recorded when Guthram the Dane captured Chippenham and spent the winter here. Alfred owned Chippenham throughout his kingship and had a palace here, probably using it as an ideal centre for hunting expeditions. The mixed fortunes of the town are well recorded but, on the whole, fate has looked kindly on this small Wiltshire town. Two notable families, the Gascelyns and the Husseys, obtained Royal Charters that made this a prosperous market town, and shortly after, the Borough became the property of the mighty Hungerford family and prospered under their powerful protection. In the Civil War Chippenham suffered much less than neighbouring Devizes and Malmesbury and the Industrial revolution was to prove advantageous to the town.

The coming of the Great Western Railway in 1850 marked a dramatic change in Chippenham. The rustic charm of a little town built entirely around its markets was shattered as the railway brought the giant markets of Bristol and London that much nearer. The firm of Saxby and Farmer set up a railway equipment factory on the edge of the town and other industries such as Warrilows Gun Works, Thomas Brotherhood and the Anglo-Swiss Canning Company increased the importance of the Borough. The town began to spread outwards engulfing the little villages of Rowden, Lowden and Cocklebury and, although progressive, the town accepted the challenge of technology without destroying the past. The town itself did not suffer and, right through to the early 1900's, this beautiful town with its exquisite buildings of local stone stood like a jewel on the line of the modern railway. How fortunate that the photographs shown in this book were taken as a permanent record for future generations. The trend over the last few decades has been to dismantle the very fabric of the old town and replace it with the concrete and glass of a more vulgar age.

If the pictures in this book stimulate an interest in our town, more details are available inside the ancient Yelde Hall which today serves as a museum of Chippenham's historic past. The museum was cared for for many years by Cecil Smith, who was a great authority on the Town's history. Cecil also provided many of the pictures in this book for which I am extremely grateful. He died in 1983 and Chippenham lost one of its finest citizens.

My thanks are due to those people who kindly loaned me postcards of Chippenham: Mr. Cecil Smith, Mr. R. Taylor, Mrs. Honour and Mr. L. Chandler.

1. This view of the High Street looking down towards the River Avon was taken in 1865. Houlstons, the booksellers on the right, being passed by the horse and cart, was the Post Office up to 1853, prior to its resiting in the Market Place. The old town bridge can be seen to the left of the picture. Notice also the classical building with tympanum which has now been replaced by 'Woolworths store', this building was dismantled stone by stone and re-erected at Kingswood School, Sion Park, in Bath where it stands to this day.

2. Looking up 'Station Hill' in 1880. Before the Great Western railway entered the town, this was known as 'Prince of Wales Hill', notice the elegant Baptist Church on the right (constructed in 1856). Also on the right, on a site now occupied by the Liberal Hall, is the ground where cattle were sold fortnightly, a practice that continued until 1930. Half way up the hill on the left is the 'Palace' cinema that continued in service until the erection of the new cinema in Timber Street in 1936. Just beyond the Palace is the postal sorting office that also owes its existence to the coming of the railway.

3. Birds Marsh at the turn of the century. This delightful spot is little changed and the picture is dated only by the elaborate fashion of the lady on the path. A beautiful wild wood with vague traces of its original role as part of a country estate, it still contains bushes of rhododendron and azaleas that, although no longer cared for, are reminders of a glorious past.

4. The River Avon was prone to flooding on a scale that we find difficult to imagine, although no great flooding was reported before 1866. October 1882 was the worst recorded and the flood of 1926, shown here, reached up the High Street as far as the Town Hall pillars where a flood mark can still be seen. The first building on the right is Pond's store, and the oriele window of 'The George' can also be seen.

5. The Great Western Hotel occupied a site between Bewley House and the railway arches and was named after the famous company that extended its railroad through Chippenham in the years 1856-1858. For almost a century it served first, the thirsty railway builders and then, later, the people of the town. It was eventually demolished in 1967 to make way for a new road development and the erection of a new Bewley House. The modern concrete edifice that serves as the headquarters of the North Wiltshire District Council.

6. In 1915 the Parish Church of St. Andrew was clearly visible from the island on the river. This Church dates back to the twelfth century and stands on a site probably occupied by a Saxon Church used by King Alfred. In 853 A.D. his sister Aethelswitha was married here to Buthred, King of the Mercians. The structure on the right of the Church is a chapel provided at the expense of the town's silk workers in 1760, aptly named after their patron saint, St. Katherine.

7. Another view of the Church from the river, this time showing the decorated ends of the Church building and the gardens of the Old Vicarage. The tower of the Church was rebuilt in 1633 following the collapse of the original through constant bell ringing, at a cost of £320. The building to the right of the picture was the National School which was erected in 1836 for the education of five hundred children of the parish.

8. Taken in 1907, this view from Cocklebury towards the town shows the Calne branch line sweeping to the left of the picture. The factory beyond the railway lines is the complex of 'Saxby and Farmer' who had bought out the existing etablishment of Evan O'Donnell in 1903, and specialised in Railway signal equipment. They were later, through a series of mergers, to become the celebrated 'Westinghouse' Company in 1935. The superimposed seal in the top right hand corner is the Borough Seal of the town still represented on the Mayor's chain of office. The school building to the left of the road was commenced in 1898 as the new Grammar school at the expense of two local charities set up by Colborne and Popham.

9. The Church of St. Paul in 1900. This Church was built in 1854 by D. Jones of Bradford-upon-Avon and designed by Giles Gilbert Scott. The foundation stone was laid by Joseph Neeld. The Church was finished ahead of the tower which is a separate construction. The Church was the result of the initiative of the Scott-Ashe family of nearby Langley-Burrell, who owned most of the surrounding land. On the extreme left a portion of the 'Little George' can be seen only three years before it was completely destroyed in a fire.

10. The Primitive Methodist Church of Lowden in 1907. Built in 1855, this building is now used as a garage by Chequers. It is difficult to imagine it as a chapel today but, on one side of the building the old chapel windows can still be clearly seen.

11. The interior of St.-Andrew's Church in the late 1800's. The insert is of Canon Maxwell Smith. In 1875 this Church was 'restored' as were so many English Churches at that time. The Hungerford chapel to the right of the picture has been extensively altered, but traces of the Hungerford family crest and shield can still be found in the Church. Notice the pews which were removed in 1973. Also, since this picture was taken, a fine carved screen has been erected in memory of the local men who died during the war. The screen carries numerous coats of arms, in particular those of Hungerford who was the town's greatest Lord.

12. The Church of Hardenhuish was designed by John Wood, the architect of Bath, and built in 1779 at the expense of Joseph Colborne Sheriff of Wiltshire. Dedicated to St. Nicholas, the Church remains little changed today except for the removal of the Ivy prominent in this picture. The stone used in its construction came from a demolished Church situated further down the hill. The memorial to the right of the Church is the grave of David Ricardo, who married one of the Clutterbuck daughters and pursued a political career as Member of Parliament for Portalington in 1819. He was a very rich Dutch Jew, who is commemorated by this magnificent marble tomb built by William Pitts, the sculpture. David Ricardo died in 1823.

13. Chippenham Market Place in 1915 is instantly recognisable even today. The buildings, a little higher than the Angel, occupy the site upon which it is said King Alfred established a Hunting Lodge. This area was, in Saxon times, a massive forest and the small settlement of Chippenham was ideally suited for hunting expeditions.

14. The Yelde Hall as it was in 1928. Probably the oldest building in the town, today it houses the town museum under the curatorship of Cecil Smith and is easily identified in this picture. The gun has long since disappeared along with the building to the left of the picture. Above the door can be seen the town seal and the initials of John Scott who was the Bailiff in 1776. At the time of this picture it was 'Home' to the borough Fire Brigade who were to occupy it until 1946, when they were moved to their present site at Dallas Road.

15. This postcard is a reproduction of an old print showing the Market Place in 1820. The well in the centre was removed in 1867 to make way for the war memorial, and the building at the rear, once the White Hart, is now a supermarket. The pump shown was purchased in 1767 for £1:15:6, and replaced an earlier one bearing the arms of the Hungerford family.

16. In 854 Hardenhuish was a Manor held by the saxon Haregeard. Hardenhuish House was built in 1774 by John Wood, architect of the Circus in Bath, and in 1791 was the scene of a tragedy when Lucy, widow of General Preston, died after her nightgown caught fire from a candle she was carrying. The porch at the main entrance was added in 1820 by Sir John Soane. In 1920, when this picture was taken, it was the home of the Clutterbuck family, who, from 1822 to 1870, had run a private school within its walls. The house was the residence of Viscount Portal until 1935 when it was purchased by the County for use as a school. The house is now part of the County school complex.

17. The town bridge in 1908 showing the slip down to the river, where the Co-op now stands and to the left, the Nestles building. The little shop in the centre of the bridge was once a turnpike and was demolished along with the bridge in 1966. Of considerable age, this bridge was widened in 1796 and a ballustrade added. Traces of this ballustrade still survive. The original bridge consisted of twenty-two arches. In the background is the Temperence Hall, erected in 1863, on the site of the 'Appollo' public house. The building was paid for by public subscription and intended as place for meeting and recreation.

18. The Bull market in the centre of the town in 1905, the end of the Yelde Hall can clearly be seen. This market in the street was condemned in 1907 by the Board of Agriculture and in 1910 the market moved to the side of the Town Hall adjacent to the Neeld Hall.

19. A similar view in 1910, the wooden hurdles have been replaced by iron posts, manufactured by Rowland Brotherhood of Foundry Lane, to which the bulls were tethered. The elegant building on the right is the Jubilee Building (constructed in 1887 to mark the jubilee of Queen Victoria) which once contained the Mayor's Parlour. This building had been used as the School of Art up to 1891 when its use was extended as the forerunner of the Technical College, established at Cocklebury in 1900.

20. A view from the bridge looking up towards the town. The first building on the right was Pond's stores, a spirit vault that was demolished in 1965. The lady wearing the cloak has been identified as Miss Maddley, a well known worker at St. Paul's Church.

21. This view down the High Street was taken about 1900. This interesting scene that shows the leisurely pace of traffic in the town. Note the shop on the left (double gabled) which was the property of Joe Buckle, who was for many years Captain of the Fire Brigade and a well known personality in the town.

22. A similar view to the last but from ground level some twenty-five years later. It is interesting to note that the double gabled building on the left, Joe Buckles shop, now appears to be half-timbered! On the right, a glimpse of the beautiful building that once occupied the site now used by Woolworths. This fine building was dismantled with great care and moved to Bath where it was re-erected as the front to Kingswood house, now a private school.

23. An excellent view of the town bridge about 1874. Showing the open site where a Charity shop now stands and beyond, the face of the Temperance Hall in Foghamshire. This building has served as a school for young ladies in 1898, a YMCA during the First World War and as a Forces Canteen during the Second World War. The horse and cart in the foreground are at the fountain supplied by Esmead for the town and bringing water from a spring on the island. This fountain is now resited and preserved outside the Yelde Hall.

24. Looking up the High Street in 1870, this fascinating picture reveals a scene of life without hurry or bustle. The largest building in the centre was an Ironmongers shop. The spire of St. Andrew's Church is visible in the top right hand corner.

25. In the summer of 1907, King Edward VII visited the town and rode in procession through the streets of Chippenham. This view, showing the crowds that turned out to greet him in the Market place, gives a good view of the old 'Talbot Inn' which was to be demolished in 1968 to make way for the present Barclay's Bank.

26. A Carnival procession also in 1907, crosses the bridge and climbs up the High Street. The Town Hall is just visible and on the extreme left, Joe Buckles shop. Just leaving the bridge is the Fire Brigade who were quartered at the Yelde Hall at this time.

27. Common slip on the River Avon, in addition to being a shallow crossing place, this was also the point at which the townswomen did their laundry. In time of flood this crossing could be treacherous and, in 1795, Samuel Fletcher rode his horse into the stream only to be swept off and drowned. This river bubbles into life at nearby Luckington and continues its journey through Bath and Bristol to join the River Severn at Avonmouth.

28. Soldiers and nurses who attended the emergency hospital for the war wounded in the Neeld Hall and Town Hall. In 1915 this emergency hospital played an important part in convalescing wounded soldiers, over 1800 wounded soldiers were treated here by the V.A.D.'s.

29. The Market Place showing the Angel Hotel in 1930. This hotel dates back to 1613, but the frontage is eighteenth century. Originally known as 'The Bull' in 1613, its name was changed sometime before 1747. The fireplace inside the Bar is part of the seventeenth century structure. In 1785 a Richard Harris fell down the stairs of the Angel and died, and in 1865 it was the scene of much commotion when windows were smashed by an angry mob trying to get at the newly elected M.P. John Neeld. Such was the ferocity of the crowd that a detachment of Coldstream Guards were sent for to subdue the rioters.

30. The Market Place from the opposite angle in 1905 and a good view of the Angel and the Bear. The Bear was constructed by a local builder, Jack Provis, about 1756 for Thomas Neate and was sold to Sir Samuel Fudyer, M.P. in 1764. Horses and sheep were sold outside on market days as late as 1910. In the background is the canal wharf, now the bus station, which belonged to Mr. W.H. Brinkworth and was opened in 1799 as the Chippenham link of the Berks and Wilts canal to connect Chippenham with the flourishing Kennet and Avon canal near Melksham. The canal closed in 1917.

31. The Buttery 1875, recently restored. This quaint structure occupied the site now covered by Barclays Bank. It was, until recently, to be found in a garden at Castle Combe. Some of the gentlemen in this picture have been identified: R. Fry (standing), E. Bradfield (seated) and two men named Thomas and Hulbert.

32. John Coles Park 1926. This park was given to the town of Chippenham at the bequest of John Coles, a prominant citizen and grocer of the Town, who was Mayor in 1891, 1898 and 1914. He left £4,000 to the Borough to purchase the land. The park was opened in 1922.

33. This huge building was constructed by the 'Anglo Swiss Condensed Milk Company' as a factory for the processing of milk. Eventually this Company became a part of the world-famous Nestles Company and became the first plant in Britain to adopt the system of packing condensed milk in cans. At its peak it was handling a hundred or more carts delivering milk per day. The Company eventually moved to nearby Staverton and the Chippenham site fell into disuse.

34. Park Lane in 1904, with the original building used by the West End Club in the foreground. This lovely building has survived, but is no longer used by the club, who have moved to new premises nearby. In the background at the top of Park Lane can be seen the spire of St. Paul's Church.

35. This picture shows the two public houses called ‘The Lamb’ and ‘The Swan’ (Paddy’s goose) flanking the gun works of John Bakewell Warrilow. Originally a silk factory, this building was adapted by Warrilow for the manufacture of extremely fine guns that were noted for the quality of their lock mechanisms. All the buildings in this picture have long since disappeared to make way for a supermarket. ‘The Lamb’ sold Dowdings ales and ‘The Swan’ had it’s own brewery. In the background can be seen the Back Avon bridge.

36. Park Lane in 1926 with the 'Little George' on the extreme left. This is the second 'Little George', the original of 1784 having burned in 1903. The building to the rear with the small tower is the St. Paul's National School which was built in 1857 on the site of a 'Dame' school.

37. Back Avon Bridge in 1910 looking up River Street. The buildings seen here were demolished in 1913 to make room for the market. This area of the river is now occupied by a modern flood control system. The river had always been dangerous but the drowning of William Deverell, who fell from the Back Avon Bridge in 1788, caused the elders of Chippenham to deliberate on the construction of a new and safer bridge at this point. However, despite these efforts William Mitchell fell from the bridge and was drowned in 1853.

38. Market Place in 1914, showing on the right the premises of John Coles, townsman and benefactor, who was Mayor of Chippenham three times. Next door is the 'English Colonial Meat Company'. John Coles came from Birmingham in 1870 and purchased 25 Market Place from Mr. J.D. Goold. He died unmarried and left £4,000 to the Borough. He became a member of the Borough Council in 1886 and was the first chairman of the Technical College in 1891.

39. Greenways House in 1900, now the Business Park, but then the house of a large estate. The house was built in 1900 by Captain Allfrey, who's son married a Miss Clutterbuck of Hardenhuish House.

40. 1880 looking down New Road from the Railway arches. St. Andrew's spire to the top left. The many advertising boards at the foot of Station Hill were a feature of Chippenham for a long time, and this site was never filled with a permanent building.

41. An interesting view of the Causeway in 1926. This has always been the main road into town from London and the surface was so bad in the coaching days that coaches from London had to divert down St. Mary Street. At this time it was known as ‘Rotten Row’. The building on the left advertising ‘Georges Bristol Beers’ was a public house called the ‘Five Alls’. It was first recorded as an Inn in 1823 and continued as such until 1937 when another public house of the same name was erected in Sheldon Road.

VISIT OF H.M. KING EDWARD VII. TO CHIPPENHAM, JULY 20th, 1907.

[Tomkins & Barrett, Swindon.

42. On the 20th of July 1907, King Edward VII visited Chippenham. This historic visit is recorded here in a splendid scene in the High Street looking up towards St. Andrew's Church. The building on the immediate left has now been replaced by the more modern premises of the Co-operative store.

43. New Road in 1932 showing the Railway arches and a train posed neatly on top. This locomotive is a Great Western Type 4800T 0-4-2 Tanker, specifically introduced for branch line working. This one is probably on the Melksham run. The arches were built by Isambard Kingdom Brunel as part of his Great Western Railway project.

44. Chippenham Bridge with the Avon in flood. The iron gates on the left are for the new cattle market, and just below, is the 'County shoe stores'. Notice the milk churns being conveyed on their way to the Nestles factory.

45. No. 21 the High Street being demolished by Rudmans in 1913. This was 'Blackfords' shop and claims to be established in 1761. Compare it with postcard number one which is dated 1865 and displays the name 'Ireland'.

46. A stage coach leaving the Angel Hotel bound for Bath. Note the badge over the door which is the badge of the 'Cyclist Touring Club' of Great Britain.

47. An interesting view of the High Street showing clearly the premises of Blackfords. Notice the elegant costume of the people which shows in vivid detail the fashion of the period. The building at the top of the picture was the retail outlet of the Royal Wilts Bacon Company.

48. This is New Road, once called 'The Marshfield Turnpike Road', looking up towards the railway bridge. The shop on the immediate left was one of many ironmongers in the town. (Due to the agricultural nature of the district, this trade was in great demand.)

49. Chippenham in flood, in this shot the Avon has burst its banks and completely covered the town bridge, reaching up the High Street as far as Robert Afflecks Iron-mongers (on the left). Such flooding was common place and disrupted the commerce of the district for many years, even as late as the 1950's. The modern flood control system has made this a thing of the past.

50. An excellent view of a typical town shop in the Market Place. Note the iron bollards used for tethering cattle on market days. This shop specialised in furniture of quality and works of Art. It also offered warehousing facilities. The shop still exists, but is now the premises of an undertaker.

BOWOOD HOUSE, CHIPPENHAM. *R. Wilkinson & Co., Photo.*

51. An unusual view of Bowood House, the residence of the Earls of Shelburne. These gardens are now open to the public, but the large block to the right of the building complex has now gone. The gallery on the left remains and contains many pictures and sculptures which are on view to the public. It was in this house that Doctor Joseph Priestley had his laboratory and, under the patronage of the first Lord Lansdowne, discovered Oxygen on the 1st August 1774.

52. Another view of John Coles stores in the Market Place. This photograph was taken for use as an advertisement in a small guide book to the town in 1910.

53. The Causeway looking towards Calne. The state of this road during the coaching era was so bad that it became known as 'Rotten Row'. Coaches used the divert down St. Mary Street to avoid it. The 'Five Alls' public house on the extreme right eventually closed in 1937 and a new 'Five Alls' openend in Sheldon Road in that same year. The building in the picture survives and is now a Chinese restaurant.

54. This fascinating picture is not easily identified but is, in fact, the front of the 'White Hart' used here as the trading premises of Heath and Son, Miliners. In 1648, when it was a thriving coaching inn, Oliver Cromwell stayed here on his way to Bristol. It seems to have strong Parliamentarian connections for, in 1650, when Cromwell was proclaimed Lord Protector of England, the Bailiff of Chippenham, Edward Hawkins, led the celebrations at the White Hart.

55. St. Andrew's Church, Jubilee Buildings and various shops in the Market Place. The Jubilee Building features strongly here even as it does today. Built to commemorate Queen Victoria's jublilee, it once served as the Mayor's parlour where the Mayor formally welcomed visitors to the town. Among the town treasures once displayed here was the regalia of the Borough Mayor.

56. This lovely old shop has changed much in over seventy years. As 'Smalls Stationary Stores' it sold, in addition to the usual stock, Grafton china bearing the Borough Arms in a variety of designs ranging in price from six-pence! An advertising slogan of 1910 read: 'The favour of your patronage is respectfully solicited.' At the rear and to the left can be seen the frontage of the 'Rose and Crown'.

57. This magnificent building no longer exists, pulled down a few years ago, only the stable block at the rear remains. Draycot was the country seat of the Long family, who have featured prominently in the history of the County. Sir James Long was a Royalist and once led a triumphant attack against the Parliamentarians in the town of Chippenham. The family died out with no male heirs and Catherine, last of the line, married into the Wellesley family, who's most notable ancestor was the Duke of Wellington.

58. Edgar Neale, Chemist, was once a familiar part of every-day life in Chippenham. Few realise that this business has operated for so many decades. This picture was taken in 1910 and at the time the stock in trade included such delights as Turtle jelly, Calfs-foot jelly and photographic plates! In those days the telephone number of the shop was 2Y!

59. The market square with the Jubilee buildings prominant on the left. The first market on this site dates back to the granting of Charters to the Gascelyn family in the fourteenth century. The sale of cattle continued in the area shown until about 1910 when such activity was transferred to the new market by the Neeld Hall. The sale of poultry continued in the old market place for some time.

60. This shop stands beside the Bear Hotel overlooking the Market Place. In the window can be seen a wonderful collection of brand-new phonographs. Mr. Spencer also offered his services as a piano tuner as well as stocking all the latest records of the day.

61. Old Lowden Village, now swallowed up by the sprawling town of Chippenham. This view is instantly recognisable and has changed little over the years. The Church (centre) is still very active and most of the buildings in this picture have survived.

THE MARKET PLACE, CHIPPENHAM. *R. Winterburn, Photo.*

62. St. Andrew's Church from the steps of the Angel Hotel. Once again the fountain features prominently. This fountain covers the spring that was once the town pump originally erected by Lord Hungerford. It is thought that it was the contamination of this spring by adjacent sewers that caused the smallpox epidemic of 1711. The fountain itself has now gone and a War Memorial was erected on this site in 1952, in memory of forty-six men of the Borough who died in the war.

63. This corner building (with a glimpse of the 'Rose and Crown' to the right) still stands proudly in the Market Place, though its function is completely changed. In 1910 it was the Drapery shop of Frank Belcher.

64. The dignified building to the left in this picture of the High Street was originally the premises of the 'Capital and Counties Bank'. Due to repeated flooding they moved to the next building up which is now Lloyds Bank. The first building being taken over as the 'Wiltshire and Dorset Bank'. Today it is still a Bank and the Chippenham home of the 'Nat West'. Across the road is the front of the Neeld Hall, built in 1834.

65. Maud Heath was a lady of some wealth who lived in the nearby village of Tytherton. On the 12th of June 1474, she made a deed of gift to enable a group of appointed trustees to maintain a causeway from Wick Hill to Chippenham. This causeway built high above the river meadow would allow the locals to get to the market of Chippenham in time of flood. This statue was erected in 1838 to commemorate this public benefactor.

66. Thomas Brotherhood, a local engineer, established a foundry in Chippenham that was to give its name to 'Foundry Lane'. After he left the premises they were taken over by the Royal Wiltshire Bacon Company and this view shows the inside of the building in use for the preparation of bacon. No less than four private railway lines ran from the nearby Great Western Railway sidings into the factory premises, one of these lines being seen in the foreground of the picture. At this period some 150 pigs per week were being processed and the factory specialised in the celebrated 'Bradenham Hams'.

67. This picture was taken from the centre of the old bridge looking towards New Road. On the extreme right can be seen the branches of the magnificent Plane tree that fell to the developers axe in 1957. The building on the extreme left was actually on the bridge itself and has long since gone. The building in the centre still stand and serves as a Charity shop.

68. It is surprising how many of Chippenham's trades have continued even though there have been changes of ownership. This shop stands across the road from the old town mill, now destroyed to make way for a parade of shops.

69. An idylic cameo of the old bridge framed by the lush foliage of the woodland that featured strongly in what is now the open spaces of Monkton Park. The wonderful Elm trees of which Wiltshire was so proud were striken by Dutch Elm Desease some years ago and carried away such scenes as this forever. This view of the peaceful Avon sums up the peace and tranquility of our town as it used to be.

70. Another view of Richardson's shop showing the proprietor posing somewhat self-consciously outside the store of which he is obviously very proud. The tall building adjoining is part of that building featured in picture number 67.

71. Outside the town are many rural villages that depended upon Chippenham for their survival. Colerne was such a village and is typical of them all. This picture of the village Post Office, built of local stone, was taken in about 1890.

72. A broad view of the bridge showing details of the arches and the sinister building of the Nestles factory on the left. The little shops on the bridge are nicely featured here. The Nestles factory was founded in 1873 and modernised in 1935 with the first Stainless Steel Condensing plant in Europe. It closed in 1966 and is converted into offices.

73. This charming spot, captured by the camera in 1892, shows the wharf of the Wilts and Berks canal at its termination in Chippenham. The building is, in fact, the rear of the 'Rose and Crown' and the little waterway is now the bus station. In the boat can be seen Major W.H. Brinkworth who owned the wharf at this time. The canal had originally been dug (1798) to bring coal from Somerset to the industries of Chippenham. It was finally filled in in 1917.

74. The old town mill stood near the bridge of which the ballustrade is clearly visible in this picture. The mill, thought to have served the community for some one thousand years, had a breast-shot wheel of some ten-feet diameter which was capable of driving nine pairs of mill stones. The mill was destroyed by fire in 1816 and the one shown here was built on the site at about that time.

75. This view is hardly recognisable at all today. The ivy-clad house with the porch on the left, was the original Bewley House which was demolished along with the Great Western Inn to make way for the new council offices in 1967. On the right can be seen the splendid 'Western Villas' which were erected by Isambard Kingdom Brunel in 1848 as residences for his staff involved in the construction of the Great Western Railway through the town. These alas, have also gone to make way for yet more government offices.

76. This view is also not easily identified but actually shows 'Chippenham Clift' as it was in about the 1920's. This is where the famous Maud Heaths causeway ended, and the white stone on the right commemorates the fact. The wall to the left contains St. Paul's churchyard and the road to the right is 'Foundry Lane' which once led to the Royal Wilts Bacon factory and the Westinghouse complex.

77. A superb view looking up the High Street in 1926. Notice the steps leading up to the town hall entrance and the large wrought iron gates now completely changed. Above the portico of the Town Hall can be seen the coat-of-arms of Joseph Neeld, who was M.P. for Chippenham many times in the nineteenth century. The coat-of-arms was paid for by public subscription.

The Library, Chippenham. Publ. by R. F. Houlston, Chippenham.

78. Houlstons Booksellers and Library in 1904. This remarkable shop, situated in the High Street, opposite to where Woolworths now stands, served the large agricultural community around Chippenham by the provision of books on loan for a modest fee. At some time in its history the shop also served as a Post Office and was responsible for producing a great many postcards of Chippenham some of which (including this one) are to be found in this book.

79. A picture taken in 1907 shows in detail the magnificent building that was the house of Mr. G.A. White for many years. In 1934 it was demolished to make way for a Woolworth store, but fortunately the entire frontage was carefully recorded by Mr. Water Rudman and dismantled stone-by-stone by Blackfords of Calne. Mr. Thos Cook (of Cooks Tours fame) purchased it and had it re-erected at Zion Hill, Bath where it still stands to this day as part of the Kingswood school.

80. This picture of the Technical School, taken in the 1920's, is instantly recognisable to generations of Chippenham people. Today the building serves as the administrative centre for the sprawling complex of the Chippenham Technical College. When it was first erected in 1898, Cocklebury was still an isolated village and the building occupied a semi-rural site on the edge of the town.

81. Sheldon Road and the Methodist Chapel in the foreground. When this picture was taken in 1904, the Ladyfield estate was still unspoilt countryside contrasting vividly with the urban development that occupies these green fields today. Notice that the men with bicycles are inside a field which is now the junction of Sheldon Road with Audley Road.

82. Hardenhuish park forms the delightful setting for this picture of the House built by the Colborne family in 1774. This photograph was taken in the 1920's when the Clutterbuck family were in residence. The Clutterbuck family at one time ran a private school at the house and today it is known to thousands of youngsters as the Hardenhuish School belonging to the County Education Authority.

83. Above: This remarkable building is to be found hidden in woodland on the eastern outskirts of the town. The original house of Spye Park was built by Sir Edward Baynton in 1650, but this was destroyed by Major Spicer when he bought the property in 1863, and erected the building shown here. The house commands superb views over the Avon valley. This postcard carries the date '12th May, 1915' and appears to commemorate a tea party!

Below: The small church of St. Anne, built on the escarpment overlooking the Avon valley and the pretty village of Lacock, was built in the nineteenth century to commemorate the birth of a son to the Gladstone family. The Gladstones lived at nearby Bowden Park and were directly related to the famous Prime-minister of that name. To the right of the picture (taken sometime about 1910) can be seen a small sixteenth century building that is known as the Conduit house from where spring water is piped down to the village of Lacock.

84. A suitable end to this collection is a picture of the town hall of ancient Chippenham. The stone building evident here (in the 1920's) has since been removed to reveal the mediaeval half-timbered Yelde Hall beneath. This building, the centre of Chippenham life for centuries, now is the home of the town museum.